MW00437370

Spiritual Weapons
to Defeat the Enemy

Other Books by Rick Renner

Dream Thieves
Dressed to Kill
Merchandising the Anointing
Living in the Combat Zone
Seducing Spirits and Doctrines of Demons
The Point of No Return
The Dynamic Duo

To order tapes by Rick Renner,
or to contact him for speaking engagements,
please write:

Rick Renner Ministries
P. O. Box 1709
Tulsa, Oklahoma 74101-9423

Spiritual Weapons to Defeat the Enemy

Overcoming the Wiles, Devices & Deception of the Devil

Rick Renner

Albury Publishing
P. O. Box 470406
Tulsa, Oklahoma 74147-0406

Unless otherwise indicated, all scriptural quotations are from the *King James Version* of the Bible.

5th Printing

Spiritual Weapons to Defeat the Enemy
Overcoming the Wiles, Devices & Deception of the Devil
ISBN 1-88008-911-4
Copyright © 1993 by
Rick Renner Ministries, Inc.
P. O. Box 1709
Tulsa, Oklahoma 74101-9423

Published by Albury Publishing
P. O. Box 470406
Tulsa, Oklahoma 74147-0406

Excerpted from *Dressed to Kill*
Copyright © 1991 by Rick Renner

Printed in the United States of America. All rights reserved under International Copyright Law. Contents and/or cover may not be reproduced in whole or in part in any form without the express written consent of the Publisher.

Table Of Contents

Preface

Many believers and partners of my ministry have expressed their joy and gratitude over *Dressed to Kill*, but wished I had a shorter version of the same material, something less than 300 pages! They wanted to be able to pick up a small book and be built up and encouraged in the same way they were when they read *Dressed to Kill*.

For this reason, I have taken the chapters which are the heart of *Dressed to Kill* and revised them to become this powerful little book, *Spiritual Weapons to Defeat the Enemy*. I pray this new book will be a blessing to you!

Spiritual Weapons
to Defeat the Enemy

Chapter One
Put on the Whole Armor!

PAUL WRITES TO THE CHURCH at Ephesus, "Put on the whole armour of God, that ye may be able to stand against the wiles of the devil" (Ephesians 6:11).

The phrase "whole armour" is taken from the Greek word *panoplia* (pan-op-lia), and it refers to a Roman soldier who is fully dressed in his armor from head to toe. Since this is the example that Paul puts before us, we must consider the full dress, the *panoplia*, of the Roman soldier.

Because of Paul's many imprisonments, this was an easy illustration for Paul to use. Standing next to these illustrious soldiers during his prison internments, Paul could see the Roman soldier's *loinbelt, huge breastplate, brutal shoes affixed with spikes, massive, full-length shield, intricate helmet, piercing sword, and long, specially tooled lance* which could be thrown a tremendous distance to hit the enemy from afar.

The Roman soldier of New Testament times basically wore these seven pieces of armor, both offensive and defensive. These pieces of weaponry can be found in our museums today.

First of all, the Roman soldier wore a *loinbelt*. Though it was the ugliest and most common piece of weaponry that the Roman soldier wore, *it was the central piece of armor that held all the other parts together*. For instance, the loinbelt held the breastplate in place; the shield rested on a clip on the side of the loinbelt; and on the other side of the loinbelt was

1

another clip on which the Roman soldier hung his massive sword when it was not in use.

The loinbelt was so ordinary that no soldier would have written home to tell his family about his new loinbelt. Yet the loinbelt was the most important piece of weaponry that the Roman soldier owned because of its importance to the other pieces of armor. Without the loinbelt, these other pieces of weaponry would have fallen off of the soldier.

In addition to the loinbelt, the Roman soldier also wore a second weapon — *a magnificent and beautiful breastplate.* The breastplate of the Roman soldier was made out of two large sheets of metal. One piece covered the front of the soldier, and the other piece covered the back, and these sheets of metal were attached at the top of the shoulders by large brass rings. Frequently these metal plates were comprised of smaller, scale-like pieces of metal, causing the breastplate to look very similar to the scales of a fish. Later on, the breast-plate was most often referred to as a "coat of mail."

This heavy piece of weaponry began at the bottom of the neck and extended down past the waist to the knees. From the waist to the knees it took on the resemblance of a skirt. The breastplate was by far the heaviest piece of equip-ment that the Roman soldier owned. Depending upon the physical stature of the soldier, this piece of equipment at times could weigh in excess of 40 pounds. In First Samuel 17:5, we are told that Goliath's breastplate weighed "five thousand shekels of brass," or the equivalent of 125 pounds!

In addition to this beautiful coat of mail, the Roman soldier also wore a third weapon — *very dangerous shoes.* These shoes were not like the Roman sandals that people wear today. The sandals people wear today are merely a flimsy little piece of twine that is wrapped around their heel and their toe.

The shoes which the Roman soldier wore were primar-ily made of two pieces of metal. The first piece of the Roman shoe was called *a greave.* This was a piece of bronze or brass that had been wrapped around the soldier's lower legs. Beginning right at the top of the knee, it extended down past the calf of the leg and rested on the top of the foot. Because this tube-like piece of metal covered the lower leg of the soldier, the Roman soldier's shoes looked like boots that were made of brass!

The top, sides and bottom of the foot were decked with a very thick piece of heavy metal. On the bottom, the Roman soldier's shoes were affixed with extremely dangerous spikes. If you were a civilian soldier, the spikes on the bottom of your shoes were approximately one inch long. If, however, you were involved in active combat, the spikes on the bottom of your shoes could be somewhere between one to three inches long. These shoes, which Paul amazingly calls "shoes of peace" in Ephesians 6:15, were intended to be "killer shoes."

In addition to these "killer shoes," the Roman soldier also carried a fourth important weapon — *a large, oblong shield*. This massive shield was made of multiple layers of animal hide that were tightly woven together, and were then framed along the edges by a strong piece of metal or wood.

The fifth weapon which the Roman soldier wore was his *helmet*. This all-important piece of armor, which protected the soldier from receiving a fatal blow to the head, at times weighed 15 pounds or more. Surprisingly, while the breastplate was the most beautiful piece of weaponry which the Roman soldier possessed, the helmet was the most noticeable. It would have been very difficult to pass by a Roman soldier without noticing his helmet.

The sixth weapon of the Roman soldier was his *sword*. While there were many kinds of swords during that time, the sword which the Roman soldier carried was a very heavy, broad and massive sword that was specifically created for jabbing and killing an adversary or foe.

And seventh, the Roman soldier carried *a specially tooled lance* that was designed to strike the enemy from a distance.

Most have not recognized the presence of the lance in Ephesians 6:10-18, but the lance must be present in the text because we are told to "put on the *whole armour* of God. . . ."

There is no doubt that the lance was a part of the whole armour of the Roman soldier. In order for Paul to carry through this illustration about the "whole armour of God," it is absolutely necessary for the lance to be included in this text. In this book, you will see that the lance is indeed a very important part of "the whole armour of God."

A New Set of Clothes!

These weapons are clearly taken from the picture of a Roman soldier who is dressed in full armor; he is *dressed to kill!* With this example before us, now Paul gives us a powerful word of instruction. He says, "Put on the whole armour of God, that ye may be able to stand against the wiles of the devil" (Ephesians 6:11).

Especially notice that Paul says, "*Put on. . . .*" The phrase "put on" is taken from the Greek word *enduo*, which is frequently used throughout the New Testament. In fact, it is the exact word Luke used when he recorded Jesus, as saying, "And behold, I send the promise of my Father upon you: but tarry ye in the city of Jerusalem until ye be endued with power from on high" (Luke 24:49).

The word *enduo* refers to the act of "putting on a new set of clothes." In light of this, one expositor has properly translated Luke 24:49, ". . . but tarry ye in the city of Jerusalem until ye be clothed with power from on high." The word *enduo* has to do with the "putting on of a new set of clothes."

Paul used the word *enduo* throughout his writings to symbolically depict the "putting on" of the new man. In both Ephesians 4:24 and Colossians 3:10, he urges us to "*put on the new man. . . .*" By using the word *enduo* in these two particular passages, Paul tells us to "put on" the new man and the fruit of our new life in the same way that one would put on a brand new set of clothes.

Now Paul uses the word *enduo* in Ephesians 6:11 in this same way (i.e., to denote the act of "putting on a new set of clothes"), only now he uses this word in connection with spiritual armor. He instructs us to *"Put on the whole armour of God. . . ."*

Moreover, he uses the *imperative tense* in this text. This means he was not making a suggestion, but rather, he was issuing the very strongest kind of command that can be given. In the strongest tone of voice available, he is commanding us with great urgency to take some kind of immediate action. This action is so important, when Paul speaks to us, he speaks in the *imperative tense* — commanding and ordering us to *"Be clothed with the whole armour of God. . . ."*

We can reject his command to "Put on the whole armour of God," or we can accept it. If we choose to take Paul's command to heart, then we must learn *how* to put on "the whole armour of God."

How Do You Put on
the Whole Armor of God?

Paul describes this weaponry as "the whole armour *of God."* Especially notice the phrase "*of God."* This little phrase is taken from the Greek phrase *tou theo* (tou the-o), and it is written in the *genitive case.*

Simply put, this means this supernatural set of weaponry comes directly *from God Himself. God is the source of origination for this armor.* Thus, we could more accurately translate this verse, "Put on the whole armor *that comes from God. . . ."*

Because this weaponry has its origination in God, it is vital for us to remain in unbroken fellowship with God in order for us to continually enjoy the benefits of this spiritual armor. By breaking fellowship with the Lord, we step away from Him, our all-important power source. But as long as our fellowship with the Lord is intact, then our power source is also intact.

I am amazed by people who ignore their spiritual lives and cease to walk in the power of God, and then complain because it seems like all kinds of trouble breaks loose in their lives! They often look for deep, dark reasons for this trouble that has erupted in their lives — when the reason for this outbreak of confusion is simple: spiritual armor has its source in God, and when you temporarily cease to walk in fellowship with the Lord and in the power of God, you are choosing to temporarily step away from the source from which this armor comes!

Just as we draw our life *from God,* and just as we draw our nature *from God,* and just as we draw our spiritual power *from God,* this spiritual armor also comes *from God.*

What happens to your spiritual life when you temporarily cease to walk in fellowship with the Lord? In that state of being, do you enjoy abundant life as you once did? *Of course not!*

While abundant life still belongs to you, this state of stagnation will pull the plug on abundant life so that you cannot enjoy it as you once did. Why? *Because abundant life has its source in the Lord!* When you temporarily cease to walk in fellowship with the Lord, you elect to temporarily walk away from that flow of abundant life.

What happens to the power of the Holy Spirit in a believer's life when they develop a "who cares" attitude about their spiritual development? Do they continue to enjoy the power of God in their life? *Certainly not!*

While the power of God is still available to that believer, this "who cares" attitude temporarily pulls the plug on their power source. Why? *Because this spiritual power has its origination in the Lord!* When you temporarily stop walking in fellowship with the Lord, you are choosing to temporarily stop the flow of this divine power into your life.

Furthermore, what happens to a believer's ability to walk in spiritual armor when they temporarily suspend their relationship with the Lord? Do they continue to reap the benefits of their God-given spiritual armor in this state of suspension? *Of course not!*

While this spiritual armor is still accessible for them to use and enjoy, by temporarily suspending their relationship with the Lord, they are opting to temporarily suspend their ability to walk in the armor of God — the very armor that God gave to protect and defend them. Why? *Because your spiritual armor has its origination in the Lord!* By putting your spiritual life temporarily "on hold," you have opted to lay your armor aside until you begin walking in fellowship with the Lord again.

Many people begin each new day by pretending to "put on the whole armour of God." When they awaken and get out of bed in the morning, the first thing they do is to act as though they are actually putting on each piece of their weaponry.

They reach down to their waist, and pretend that they are actually wrapping the loinbelt of truth around them; they reach to their chest and carry on as though they are actually placing a breastplate of righteousness across their upper torso; they manipulate their feet as though they are really putting shoes of peace on their feet; they reach over and act as though they are really picking up a shield of faith to carry throughout the day; they pretend to put on a helmet of salvation; and they simulate the movements of one who is placing a sword in its scabbard along their side.

While this daily routine is fine to do, and may help some people to focus better on their spiritual life (especially children), this daily simulation of putting on a suit of armor does not put "the whole armour of God" on anyone.

The armour of God is ours by virtue of our relationship with God! Thus, the reason that Paul wrote in the genitive case. He wanted us to know that this armor originates in God, and is freely bestowed upon those who continually draw their life and existence from God. *Your unbroken, ongoing relationship with God is your absolute guarantee that you are constantly and habitually dressed in "the whole armour of God."*

Also notice that in Ephesians 6:11, Paul says, "Put on the *whole armour* of God. . . ." God has not provided a partial set of weaponry for us; He has provided a complete set of weaponry for us. He has given us "the *whole armour* of God."

Again, the phrase "whole armour" is taken from the word *panoplia* and pictures a Roman soldier that is fully dressed in his armor from head to toe. Everything the soldier needed to successfully combat his adversary was at his disposal; likewise, God has given us *everything* we need to successfully combat opposing spiritual forces! *Nothing is lacking!*

It is unfortunate that some denominations and Charismatic organizations have majored only on certain parts of the armor of God. Some teach incessantly on "the shield of faith" and the "sword of the Spirit" and neglect the other pieces of armor which God has given us. Other groups and denominations seem to preach and teach on nothing but the "helmet of salvation" week after week. They have their helmets on, *but otherwise they are stark naked!* We are commanded to "put on the *whole armour* of God. . . ."

Thank God for our loinbelt of truth, *but God gave us more than a loinbelt. . .* Thank God for our breastplate, *but God gave us more than a breastplate. . .* Thank God for our shoes of peace, *but God gave us more than shoes of peace. . .* Thank God for our shield, *but God gave us more than a shield. . .* Praise God for our helmet, *but God gave us more than a helmet. . .*and thank God for our sword of the Spirit, *but we have been given more than the sword of the Spirit!*

We have been given "the *whole armour* of God!" It is this armor that Paul commands us to pick up and use in the course of our Christian lives!

Chapter Two
Understanding Your Enemy

A S PAUL CONTINUES in Ephesians 6:11, he tells us "why" we need this armor. He says, "Put on the whole armour of God, *that ye may be able to stand against the wiles of the devil.*"

You should especially notice the phrase, ". . . that ye may be *able*. . . ." The word "able" is from the word *dunamis* (du-na-mis), and it describes "explosive ability, dynamic strength or power." This Greek phrase could be more accurately translated, ". . . *that you may have incredible, explosive, dynamic power*. . . ." By using this word, Paul declares that when we are equipped with "the whole armour of God," we have explosive and dynamic power at our command!

This *dunamis* power is so strong that, when we are walking in the whole armor of God, for the first time in our lives, we are equipped to confront and pursue the enemy, rather than be pursued by him. Because of this *dunamis* power that is at our command, we become the aggressors! This is why Paul continued to say, ". . . that ye may be able to *stand against*. . . ."

The phrase "to stand" is taken from the word *stenai* (ste-nai), and it literally means "to stand." In this verse, Paul uses the word *stenai* to picture a Roman soldier who is standing upright and tall, with his shoulders thrown back, and his head lifted high. This is the image of a proud and confident soldier, and not one who is slumped over in defeat and despondency.

9

This word *stenai* ("to stand") depicts what we look like to the spirit realm when are walking in "the whole armour of God." This armor puts us in a winning position! There is no reason for us to live our lives slumped over in defeat. *We are equipped to beat the living daylights out of any foe that would dare assault us.*

Hence, we can walk boldly and confidently — with our shoulders thrown back, and our head lifted high; because we are dressed in "the whole armour of God!"

There is something else important about this word *stenai* which must be pointed out. The word *stenai* was used in a military sense to mean "to maintain a critical and strategic military position over a battlefield." Why is this so important? Because this meaning of *stenai* implies that we have a responsibility "to stand guard" over the battlefields of our own lives!

If God has called you and given you a specific job to do in the Body of Christ, then you must "stand guard" and "maintain a critical position" over that job until it is fulfilled. The devil does not want you to fulfill the call of God upon your life. He may try to attack that call from God, and turn it into a battlefield. Therefore, until the job is finished and the battle is won, you must "stand guard" over the will of God for your life. You must determine that you will not give the enemy an inch! This is your responsibility!

The most important battlefield of your life is your mind! Spiritual warfare is primarily a matter of the mind. As long as the mind is held in check and is renewed to right thinking by the Word of God, the majority of spiritual attacks will fail. However, when the mind is left open and unguarded, it becomes the primary battlefield that Satan uses to destroy lives, finances, businesses, marriages, emotions, and so on. It is your responsibility to "stand guard" over these areas of your life!

An Eyeball-to-Eyeball Confrontation!

Please notice the next word in this verse! Paul continues, ". . . that ye may be able to stand *against*. . . ." The word "against" is derived from the word *pros* and it denotes a "forward position" or "a face-to-face encounter."

By employing the word *pros* in this verse, Paul is portraying the picture of a soldier who is looking his enemy directly in the face — *eyeball to eyeball!* This is a soldier that is standing tall; his shoulders are thrown back, and his head is lifted high; he is so bold, daring and courageous, that he is now fearlessly glaring right into the eyes of his adversary. The word *pros* undoubtably depicts an *eyeball-to-eyeball confrontation!*

This clearly demonstrates that, with the power of God and the armor of God on our side, we are more than a match for the enemy! Moreover, we are a fearsome and terrible plight to his domain! Rather than shudder at the thought of what the devil can do to us, this spiritual armor puts us in a super-powerful position to make the devil shudder and tremble at the thought of what we can do to him!

With this armor of God in hand, we are so mighty and powerful in Jesus Christ, that the devil and his forces are no match for us! When we are dressed in this suit of armor, we become mighty spiritual warriors who are "dressed to kill!"

Taking a Stand Against the Wiles of the Devil

Why do we need this armor? What are we supposed to "stand against" in this conflict? Paul tells us, "Put on the whole armour of God, that ye may be able to stand against *the wiles of the devil*" (Ephesians 6:11).

What are "the wiles of the devil?"

The word "wiles" is one of three key words which you must know and understand when discussing the subject of spiritual warfare. These three key words are: (1) *"wiles,"* (2) *"devices,"* and (3) *"deception."* It is impossible to have a

11

correct and balanced view of spiritual warfare without having an understanding of these three foundational words.

The word "wiles" (the first of these three words) is taken from the Greek word *methodos* (meth-o-dos). It is a compound of the words *meta* (me-ta) and *odos* (pronounced ho-dos). The word *meta* is a preposition which simply means "with." The word *odos* is the Greek word for a "road." By compounding these two words into one, they form the word *methodos*. Literally translated, the Greek word *methodos* means "with a road."

It is from this word *methodos* that we derive the word "method." But the English word "method" is not really strong enough to convey the full meaning of *methodos* ("wiles"). The word *methodos* was carefully selected by the Holy Spirit because it tells us *exactly* how the devil operates, and it tells us *exactly* how he comes to attack and assault a believer's mind.

The word "wiles" (methodos) is often translated to carry the idea of something that is "cunning, crafty, subtle or full of trickery." However, in its most literal sense, the word *methodos* means "with a road." So the most basic translation of the word "wiles" is simply "with a road."

By electing to use this word, Paul tells us how the devil puts his cunning, crafty, subtle, and tricky deception to work! The word "wiles" plainly tells us that the devil operates "with a road" or "on a road." *What does this mean?*

Contrary to the common belief of most people, this means that the devil *does not* have as many tricks in his bag as he would have you to believe. The word "wiles" *(methodos)* plainly means that the enemy travels on *one road;* he travels on *one lane;* or he travels on *one avenue.* In other words, he primarily has only *one trick* in his bag — and he obviously has learned to use that *one trick* very well!

"What is that one trick that the devil uses against people?" Or perhaps we should more correctly ask, "If the devil operates on one single avenue of travel, where is that diabolical road headed toward?" These questions lead us to the second important word to understand when discussing spiritual warfare: the word *"devices."*

The Devices of the Devil

In Second Corinthians 2:11, Paul gives us a clue as to where this road the devil is traveling on is headed. He says, ". . . we are not ignorant of Satan's *devices."*

The word "devices" is taken from the word *noemata* (no-e-ma-ta), which is derived from the word *nous* (pronounced noous). The word *nous* is the Greek word for the "mind" or the "intellect." However, the form *noemata*, as used by Paul in Second Corinthians 2:11, carries out the idea of a *deceived mind.* Specifically, this word *noemata* denotes the insidious and malevolent plot of Satan to fill the human mind with "confusion."

The word "devices" *(noemata)* actually depicts the "insidious plots" and "wicked schemes" of Satan to attack and victimize the human mind. One expositor has even stated that the word "devices" bears the notion of *"mind games."* With this idea of "mind games" in mind, you could translate the verse, ". . . *we are not ignorant of the mind games that Satan tries to pull on us."*

Because Paul used this word "devices" to describe attacks which he, himself, had resisted, we know that even Paul had to deal with the mental assaults of the adversary from time to time. Even Paul knew about the "mind games" which the devil tries to pull on people!

It was for this very reason that Paul said, "Casting down *imaginations,* and every high thing that exalteth itself against the knowledge of God, and bringing into captivity every thought to the obedience of Christ" (Second Corinthians 10:5).

The devil loves to make a playground out of people's minds! He delights in filling their emotions and senses with illusions that captivate their minds and ultimately destroy them. He is a master when it comes to "mind games."

Like Paul, we must make a mental decision to take charge of our minds and "take every thought captive to the obedience of Christ." *We must stop listening to ourselves, and start speaking to ourselves!*

The devil always tries to manipulate our emotions and senses in order to pull a "mind game" on us. Therefore, we must speak to our emotions and senses, and we must dictate to them and tell them what to believe!

By considering the words "wiles" and "devices," we have now seen two vitally important things which we *must* know about the devil's strategy to attack and victimize the human mind.

First, the word "wiles" *(methodos)* explicitly tells us that the devil travels "with a road" or "on a road." This road which the devil is traveling on is obviously headed somewhere! *Where is that road headed?*

The word "devices" clearly demonstrates that this road of the devil is headed toward *the mind.* Whoever controls the mind, also controls that person's health and emotions. The enemy knows this! Therefore, he seeks to penetrate our intellect, our mental control center, so that he may flood it with deception and falsehood. Once this is accomplished, then from this position of control, the devil can begin to manipulate that person's body and emotions.

When this penetration into the mind is accomplished, and once the adversary has paved a road into that person's mind and emotions, the process of mental and spiritual captivity is well under way. If this devilish process is not aborted by the power of God, and by the renewing of the mind, it is only a matter of time before a solid stronghold of deception will begin to dominate and manipulate that person's self-image, emotional status and his overall thinking.

This leads us to the third word which we must understand when discussing spiritual warfare: the word *"deception."*

The Deception of the Devil

Deception occurs when a person believes the lies that the enemy has been telling him. The moment you begin to believe the lie that the devil has been telling you, is the very moment when those wicked thoughts and mind games begin to produce reality in your life.

The devil may assault your mind by repeatedly telling you that you are a failure. However, as long as you resist those allegations, they will exert absolutely no power in your life.

If, on the other hand, you begin to give credence to these lies and mentally perceive them as though they are really the truth, those lies will begin to dictate to you and will dominate your emotions and your thinking. In the end, your faith in that lie will give power to it, and will cause it to become a bona fide reality in your life; *and you will become a failure.* This is completed deception.

Many marriages fail because of allegations that the enemy tries to pound into the mind. As long as those allegations are repelled, they exert no power in that marriage. However, when a spouse pays attention to those lies and begins to dwell on them, they have taken the first fatal step toward deception.

For instance, though their marriage is in tip-top shape, a spouse may begin to have unjustified questions and suspicions about their marriage. This is clearly the work of the enemy to deteriorate one's confidence in his or her marriage. At first, the husband or wife absolutely knows that this is an outright lie of the devil. Indeed, their marriage has never been better! Yet, the enemy continues to pound away at his or her mind, *"Your spouse isn't pleased with you. . ."*

"Your marriage is in trouble. . ." "This relationship can never last. . ." "It's too good to be true. . ."

By listening to those insinuations and giving credence to them, this dear Christian sadly opens the door for the devil to continue pounding away at the mind and to prey on his or her emotions. After a period of time, if the mind, battered and weary from worrying, begins to believe these lying allegations, their belief in those lying emotions and suspicions may empower them to become a reality.

By mentally embracing such lying emotions, the believer opens a door for the enemy to penetrate his or her mind, and thus, the process of confusion is implemented; mind games are set in motion; and that believer's perception of things becomes twisted and bent.

If this seducing, deceiving process is not stopped at this point, it is probably only a matter of time before this weary- minded believer begins to embrace these mental lies as though they are really the truth.

What is the end result of all this? By falsely believing that his or her marriage is a failure; by falsely believing that his or her marriage is on the rocks; by falsely believing that they will die of a terminal disease; by falsely believing that they have no future; this believer opens the door for the devil to take these suggestions, and move them from the thought realm into the natural realm, where they become a bona fide reality. *Their false perception empowered the lie, and the devil uses that false belief to create!*

Perhaps the enemy has constantly bombarded your mind about sickness. Perhaps his lying allegations have repeatedly told you that you are going to contract a terrible disease and die an early death. When these lies first assaulted your mind, you resisted them and refused to believe what you were hearing. Now, however, you have begun to wonder if these thoughts may have some validity.

If this process is not stopped, it will only be a matter of time until you truly begin to feel physically sick in your body. Do not give credence to those lying insinuations! When you embrace those "mind games" and perceive them as truth, you give power to them! Thus, if you do not speak to yourself and take charge of your mind, the complete process of deception will continue working in your life, until finally, the process is complete and your fears become reality. *When this occurs, you are deceived.*

So these three things — *the wiles, devices and deception of the devil* — are extremely important for us to see and understand, especially when studying the subject of spiritual warfare.

For review, the word *"wiles" (methodos)* tells us that the devil operates "with a road" or primarily with "one avenue" of attack.

Secondly, the word *"devices" (noemata)* tells us where that avenue is headed: It is headed toward *the mind.* Once that road is paved into the mind, the enemy begins to regularly travel in and out of one's mind and emotions to confuse and scramble the mind with wrong thinking, wrong believing and false perceptions.

In the third place, *"deception"* occurs when you embrace that lie that the devil is telling you. This false perception which you have embraced will empower that lie to become a bona fide reality in your life. *This is completed deception.*

Chapter Three
Cutting Off the Giant's Head

PERHAPS THE BEST BIBLICAL EXAMPLE of the *wiles, devices and deceptions* of the devil can be found in the story of David and Goliath.

By studying the true-life story of David and Goliath, you will see all *three* of these negative forces at work, and you will see how the devil used lying allegations to intimidate the armies of Israel so that they were functionally paralyzed for forty days — until David came along with the power of God to challenge those lying allegations!

In First Samuel, chapter seventeen, the devil used Goliath to intimidate and confuse the armies of Israel for forty days. His outlandish, arrogant, boastful and proud declarations of their demise were so effective, that not one soldier from the Hebrew camp was willing to stand up to this aggressor!

The Word says, "And the Philistines stood on a mountain on the one side, and the Israelites stood on a mountain on the other side: and there was a valley between them. *And there went out a champion out of the camp of the Philistines, named Goliath, of Gath, whose height was six cubits and a span"* (First Samuel 17:3,4).

No wonder the Israelites were intimidated by Goliath! The appearance of this giant alone would be intellectually and emotionally overwhelming. Goliath was six cubits and a span tall, which is 9 feet 9 inches tall!

The next verses say, *"And he had a helmet of brass upon his head, and he was armed with a coat of mail; and the weight of the coat was five thousand shekels of brass. And he had greaves of brass upon his legs, and a target of brass between his shoulders. And the staff of his spear was like a weaver's beam; and his spear's head weighed six hundred shekels of iron; and one bearing a shield went before him"* (verses 5-7).

Goliath was armed to the max! Notice that the "coat of mail" he wore weighed "five thousand shekels of brass." Remember, five thousand shekels of brass is *the equivalent of 125 pounds!*

In addition to this helmet and this breastplate that weighed 125 pounds, he had greaves of brass and a target of brass between his shoulders! The staff of his spear was like a weaver's beam — *which means the long staff of his spear weighed at least 17 pounds.* Additionally, the scripture specifically says that the spear's head weighed six hundred shekels of iron — *which is the equivalent of 16 pounds.*

One scholar has speculated that the weight of all of these pieces of weaponry together — his helmet, breastplate, greaves, target of brass, spear, and shield — *may have weighed in excess of 700 pounds!* In every respect imaginable, Goliath was a very frightful sight! How would you feel if you were challenged by a foe who stood 9 feet 9 inches tall, and who wore in excess of 700 pounds of weaponry! If he wore weaponry that was 700 pounds in weight, imagine how much Goliath himself must have weighed!

Yet it wasn't this weaponry or Goliath's size that caused the Israelites to shrink back in fear. Then what caused the Israelites to fear? *It was the constant threats and mental bombardment that Goliath hit them with every single day. This mental harassment crippled them so that they lost sight of the awesome ability of God.*

Concerning these continuous threats of Goliath, the Word says, *"And he stood and cried unto the armies of Israel, and said unto them, Why are ye come out to set your battle in array?*

Am I now a Philistine, and ye servants to Saul? Choose you a man for you and let him come down to me. . . . If he be able to fight with me, and to kill me, then will we be your servants: but if I prevail against him, and kill him, then shall ye be our servants, and serve us. . . . And the Philistine said, I defy the armies of Israel this day; give me a man, that we may fight together" (verses 8-10).

These threats from the huge and menacing Goliath were so emotionally overpowering, that the next verse declares, *"When Saul and all Israel heard those words of the Philistine, they were dismayed, and greatly afraid"* (verse 11).

Goliath mentally and emotionally immobilized the armies of Israel without ever using a sword or spear! With words alone, he incapacitated, disabled, stunned, numbed and disarmed them. His flagrant and preposterous distortion of his own greatness was so outrageous, that his words bewitched the listening Israelite army until they were spellbound under his verbal control.

Goliath said to them, *"Who do you think you are to fight with me? Come on, just try to do damage to me, and you'll find out what I'll do to you! What's wrong? Are you afraid to face me and take me on?"*

Where do you suppose Goliath learned this kind of foul behavior? From the devil! The devil is a slanderer and an accuser! The devil seeks to incapacitate, disable, stun, numb and disarm believers today in the same way. The devil's flagrant and preposterous allegations are so outrageous, that they often bewitch listening believers until they become spellbound under the devil's control.

This outrageous conduct is still the mental tool which the devil still uses to assault the minds of believers. He verbally threatens them, *"I'll show you who the tough guy really is . . . I'll beat the living daylights out of you. . . I'll strike you down so hard and fast that you won't know what hit you. . ."*

These lying accusations are attempts of the enemy to beat a hole through your mind and emotions, so that you cannot think rationally. He comes to pave a road of fear into your mind, and then fills your mind with fear and confusion ("mind games"), so that you eventually will not have the courage you need to step out in faith to obey God with your life.

One slanderous accusation after another, the devil slanders, accuses and belittles you; he defames, maligns, reviles and smears your faith in order to drive you back into the ditch of self-preservation, where you will never do anything significant for the kingdom of God.

If you meditate and consider the devil's threats long enough, just like the children of Israel, who listened to the words of Goliath and were functionally paralyzed by fear for forty days, you will be *"dismayed and greatly afraid."* You'll find yourself living on the low side of victory, afraid to take on any new challenges — for fear that you will fail, for fear of what others will say, for fear of potential catastrophe, for fear, fear, fear, etc.

The devil wants to take you captive and destroy you with the same tools that Goliath used against the Israelites. He wants to ruin your effectiveness with mere suggestions and lying allegations!

The Hard Facts of Spiritual Warfare

Goliath did make one statement that was true! He said, *"If you are able to fight me and win, we will serve you for the rest of our lives. . . but if we win, you will serve us!"*

These battle rules that Goliath laid out were the hard facts of warfare during David's day. Whoever challenged the aggressor and won was the champion. Whoever fell in defeat would forever serve the other as a slave. These hard facts of battle are still the rules of spiritual warfare today.

If you conquer those lying emotions, slanderous accusations and deceiving suggestions that the devil tries to use in his attempt to neutralize you, then you will be able to keep the enemy in a subordinate position for the rest of your life. Having pulled the plug on his intimidating threats and boasts, he will no longer be able to take your mind captive.

If, however, you do not learn how to take your thoughts captive, your mind and emotions will be used as a tool of Satan to dominate your thought processes for the rest of your life. If you do not take charge of your mind — *if you do not learn how to speak to yourself, rather than listen to yourself* — the devil will continue to use lying emotions and illusions to manipulate, dominate and control you for the rest of your life.

Notice that Goliath said, "I defy the armies of Israel this day. . . ." The devil is still breathing out these same blasphemous and terrorizing statements: *"Just try to walk in divine health! I defy you to believe that your financial situation is going to turn around! I defy you to go into the ministry! I defy the armies of God!"*

Though the wicked Philistines never lifted a sword; they never threw a spear; and though they never budged from their encampment; they conquered the people of God — with mental and verbal terrorization and intimidation. Because Israel wrongly considered and meditated on these threats from Goliath, and allowed these thoughts to flood them with fear, they were neutralized without a ground war ever taking place.

How often did Goliath come to make these threats? The Word says, "And the Philistine drew near *morning and evening*, and presented himself forty days" (verse 16). Day and night, morning and evening, Goliath came to mentally undo the people of God.

This, of course, is how the enemy still attacks the mind and human emotions. He doesn't strike once, and then come back to strike a week later. No, instead, he strikes fast and repeatedly — again, again and again. Morning and evening he comes to try to damage faith and confidence irreparably.

The Flesh Counts for Nothing

The story goes on to say, "Now David was the son of that Ephrathite of Bethlehem-Judah, whose name was Jesse. . . he had eight sons. . . and David was the youngest: and the three eldest followed Saul. But David went and returned from Saul to feed his father's sheep at Bethlehem" (First Samuel 17:12-15).

It continues to say, "And David rose up early in the morning, and left the sheep with a keeper, and took, and went, as Jesse had commanded him [to take food to his brothers]; and he came to the trench. . . . and behold, there came up the champion, the Philistine of Gath, Goliath by name, out of the armies of the Philistines, and spake according to the same words: *and David heard them*" (verses 20-23).

Notice that it says, ". . . *and David heard them.*" This was David's first encounter with the foreboding giant! Something in Goliath's words incited anger in David's soul. What a shock it was for this young shepherd to hear a pagan Philistine insulting the God of Israel — and to see no one doing anything about it! Not only were they doing nothing about it, the next verse says, "And all the men of Israel, when they saw the man, fled from him, and were sore afraid" (verse 24).

David was so annoyed by this Philistine's verbal arrogance, that "David spake to the men that stood by him, saying, What shall be done to that man that killeth the Philistine, and taketh away the reproach from Israel? For who is this uncircumcised Philistine, that he should defy the armies of the living God?" (verse 26).

Immediately, David's elder brother was offended by David's confidence, and reprimanded him for acting too boldly. "And Eliab, his eldest brother heard when he spake unto the men; and Eliab's anger was kindled against David, and he said, Why camest thou down hither? And with whom hath thou left the sheep in the wilderness? I know

24

thy pride, and the naughtiness of thine heart; for thou art come down that thou mightiest see the battle" (verse 28).

Quite often when young men and women of God step out to challenge the foe, they are accused of acting too boldly. Our elder leaders are correct in pointing out that there is a vast difference between boldness, rudeness and arrogance. However, there is a true boldness which the Holy Spirit gives to surrendered vessels. David was so surrendered to the power of the Holy Spirit, that this Holy Spirit-inspired confidence rose up within him, and he simply could not hold this divine anger back!

In fact, David was so filled with confidence in God, and was so stunned by the fear that huge Israelite soldiers were possessed with, that he said, "What have I now done? Is there not a cause? And he turned from him toward another, and spake after the same manner; and the people answered him against after the former manner" (verse 29).

This is the picture of David saying, *"Isn't there a cause here that is worth fighting for? Isn't there a man in this camp who is man enough to face this uncircumcised Philistine? Why aren't we fighting?"*

David apparently began to turn from one soldier, and then to another, saying, *"How about you? Will you fight Goliath?"* Then he turned to another, saying, *"And how about you? Will you fight Goliath?"* Yet it is clear that no one had the faith or courage to believe this vile giant could be killed.

David's confidence and boldness immediately spread through the camp like wildfire. Likewise, you can be sure that when you determine to move in the power of God and to pull strongholds down from your life, it will make news! Everyone around you will discuss your boldness — and may even try to talk you out of it!

Notice that the Word says, "And when the words were heard which David spake, they rehearsed them before Saul, and he sent for him. And David said to Saul, Let no man's heart fail because of him; thy servant will go and fight with this Philistine" (verses 31,32).

There was a willingness in David's heart to be used of God, and to see the enemy slain. Saul was so amazed by this supernatural courage, that he said unto David, "Thou art not able to go against this Philistine to fight with him: for thou art but a youth, and he a man of war from his youth" (verse 33).

Naturally speaking, David was too young and unskilled in the natural weapons of warfare to do battle with this giant. Saul knew this. Therefore, looking on things from a natural, fleshly and worldly appearance, he knew that David — *naturally speaking* — was no match for Goliath!

But David knew the outward man — the flesh — counted for nothing when it came to moving in the supernatural power of God! He told Saul, "Thy servant kept his father's sheep, and there came a lion, and a bear, and took a lamb out of the flock. *And I went out after him...*" (verses 34,35).

Goliath is not the first enemy David has faced in life — he has already had an eyeball-to-eyeball confrontation with a lion and a bear! He was determined that those devourers were not going to steal one thing from his property — not one! David had the attitude that was necessary to defeat his enemy every time his enemy struck.

We must have this same attitude when the devil comes to manipulate our minds and emotions, when the enemy comes to strike family members with disease, when the devil clearly has come to devour our finances, or when the enemy has come to internally destroy a church or ministry.

Our attitude must be, "*Satan, you cannot have this ministry! Devil, you cannot have our finances! You cannot kill our family with sickness or disease! You cannot, cannot, cannot!*"

If the enemy does not willingly release those things when we tell him to do so, then, like David, we must "go out after him" and forcibly make him release those things which he has seized against our wills. David said, "I went out after him, and delivered it out of his mouth: and when he arose against me, I caught him by the beard, and smote him, and slew him: thy servant slew the lion and the bear. . ." (verses 35,36).

David had already experienced so much of God's power and victory in his life, that this Philistine was no threat to him! He already faced a ferocious lion — *and saw the faithfulness of God as the lion was killed.* He already faced a bear — *and saw the faithfulness of God as the bear was killed.*

Now, looking backward upon his past, and reflecting on the goodness of God that had already been bestowed upon his life, he looked straight into the face of this conflict with Goliath and said, "Thy servant slew both the lion and the bear: *and this uncircumcised Philistine shall be as one of them, seeing he hath defied the armies of the living God"* (verse 36).

David said moreover, *"The Lord that delivered me out of the paw of the lion, and out of the paw of the bear, He will deliver me out of the hand of this Philistine.* And Saul said unto David, *Go, and the Lord be with thee"* (verse 37).

Moving Beyond the Flesh

Notice Saul's response to David's desire to be used of God! The Word says, "And Saul armed David with his armour, and he put an helmet of brass upon his head; also he armed him with a coat of mail. And David girded his sword upon his armour. . ." (verses 38,39).

David had already killed the lion and the bear without the use of any natural armor or weaponry. However, because of the size of this menacing Goliath, Saul felt that David needed more than God's faithfulness!

It was as though Saul said, *"David, this fight with Goliath is going to be far more intense than your conflict with the lion and the bear, so let me help you! Let me put a helmet upon your head, and dress you in a coat of mail. Here, take my sword with you and use it as if it is your own!"*

Can you imagine how silly little David must have looked in Saul's massive armor? You can be sure that Saul's intentions were pure. He wanted David to be safe and adequately equipped with armor that was equal to Goliath's. However, Saul's counsel was extremely defective. David had never worn such armor before, and had he gone to battle with this heavy armor upon him, he would have been so weighed down by it all that he would have been unable to successfully wage warfare.

Thus, the reason that the Word continues to say, ". . . and he assayed to go; for he had not proved it. And David said unto Saul, I cannot go with these; for I have not proven them. And David put them off him" (verse 39).

Previous to this time, David had defeated his enemies without fleshly weapons. Knowing that he was unaccustomed to these kinds of fleshly weapons, and knowing that they would do him no good, he put them off and "took his staff in his hand, and chose him five smooth stones out of the brook, and put them in a shepherd's bag which he had, even in a scrip; and his sling was in his hand, *and he drew near to the Philistine*" (verse 40).

Notice it says that David "drew near to the Philistine." David, a small boy in his teenage years, charges a giant with 700 pounds of weaponry, and has nothing in hand to kill this giant, but a sling and five stones!

According to the natural man, David was not equipped to fight this kind of foe. But according to the spirit realm, David was dressed in the armor of God and was empowered by the power of God. Goliath could not see these spiritual weapons with his physical eyes. Therefore, he had no idea that David was "dressed to kill."

Verse 41 says, "And the Philistine came on and drew near unto David; and the man that bare the shield went before him. And when the Philistine looked about, and saw David, he disdained him: [i.e., he made fun of him] for he was but a youth, and ruddy, and of a fair countenance. And the

Philistine said unto David, Am I a dog, that thou comest to me with staves? And the Philistine cursed David by his gods."

Goliath was expecting more! He thought the Israelites had finally found a match for him. This is the reason that the man who bore his shield went before him; this shieldbearer was to protect Goliath from the blows of his challenger. But when Goliath looked around and saw little, young David, he was shocked! Immediately, he began to mock David and mock God!

Goliath, just like the devil does today, began to use his tools of mental and verbal harassment! Attempting to intimidate David and paralyze him with fear, the Word says, "And the Philistine said unto David, Come to me, and I will give thy flesh unto the fowls of the air, and to the beasts of the field" (verse 44).

Just as the entire army of Israel had been functionally immobilized for forty days by Goliath's outrageous claims, now Goliath was proceeding in his same course of action: *to immobilize and paralyze David with preposterous and bloated boasts and lying allegations!*

If David turned his eyes from the Lord, and stopped meditating on the faithfulness of God, and hence started considering what Goliath had to say, these threats would have immobilized him as they had immobilized the armies of Israel.

Before these threats had an opportunity to take root in his soul, and thus produce paralyzing fear, David said, "Thou comest to me with a sword, and with a shield; but I come to thee in the name of the Lord of hosts, the God of the armies of Israel, whom thou has defied" (verse 45).

He continued, "This day the Lord will deliver you into mine hand; and I will smite thee, and take thine head from thee; and I will give the carcasses of the host of the Philistines this day unto the beasts of the earth; that all the earth may know that there is a God in Israel. And all this assembly shall know that the Lord saveth not with sword and spear: for the battle is the Lord's, and He will give you into our hands" (verses 46,47).

Prevailing Over the Philistines in Your Life

Once David made his declaration of war, he wasted no time. Verse 48 says, "And it came to pass, when the Philistine arose, and came and drew nigh to David, *that David hasted. . . ."*

This must have *shocked* Goliath! Most challengers ran away from him, but David *"hasted."* In other words, *when the moment of conflict finally came, David picked up his sling and his five stones and ran toward Goliath.* When David saw Goliath coming, it was almost as though David said, "Now the action begins!"

The Word continues to say, "And David put his hand in his bag, and took thence a stone, and slang it, and smote the Philistine in his forehead, that the stone sunk into his forehead; and he fell upon his face to the earth. *So David prevailed over the Philistine with a sling and with a stone, and smote the Philistine, and slew him. . ."* (verses 49,50).

But wait . . . David wasn't finished yet! While Goliath had his face to the ground and was stunned by this small pebble that had been hurled from David's sling, David seized the opportunity to make sure the job was finished!

The story continues, *". . . but there was no sword in the hand of David. Therefore, David ran, and stood upon the Philistine, took his sword, drew it out of the sheath thereof, and slew him, and cut off his head therewith. And when the Philistines saw their champion was dead, they fled"* (verses 50,51).

Are you tired of the Philistines in your life? Are you tired of being mentally harassed and emotionally tormented by the lying insinuations and slanderous accusations of the adversary? How would you like to sling a stone into the head of those accusing thoughts, drop them to the ground, stun them, and then cut off their heads so they will cease harassing you?

This is precisely why Paul urges us, *"Put on the whole armour of God, that ye may be able to stand against the wiles of the devil."*

While natural training and education is good, and we need to get as much of it as we possibly can, eventually we all come to a place where we discover that natural weapons and natural education will not help us in our fight with unseen, spiritual enemies.

In such moments, we must move beyond the flesh, over into the realm of spiritual armor. This armor will empower any believer to successfully *"stand against the wiles of the devil."*

The Devil: His Mode of Operation

It would be a great injustice to conclude this chapter without explaining what the name "devil" means. Once you have an understanding of this name, then you will know that it was the nature of the devil, himself, that was working through Goliath to intimidate the armies of Israel.

The name "devil" is taken from the Greek word *diabolos* (dia-bo-los), and is a compound of the words *dia* and *ballo*. The word *dia* carries the idea of "penetration" and the word *ballo* means "to throw" something, like a ball or a rock.

Literally, the word *diabalos* describes the repetitive action of *hitting something again, again, again and again,* until finally the wall or membrane is so worn down that *it can be completely and thoroughly penetrated.*

Thus, the name "devil" *(diabolos)* is not only a proper name for this archenemy of the faith, but it also denotes his mode of operation. *The devil is one who strikes repeatedly — again, again and again, until he finally breaks down one's mental resistance. When this mental resistance has been broken down, then he strikes with all of his fury to penetrate the mind and to take that person's mind and emotions captive.*

31

This is how the enemy works! He repeatedly hits you with lies, suggestions, accusations, allegations and one slanderous assault after another, another and another. He tries to wear you down, and then takes you captive in one of your weaker moments.

He tries to pave a road into your mind *(methodos)*, and then confuse your emotions with "mind games" *(noemata)*, and then deceives you to the point that you actually begin to believe his threats — and thus, your false perception empowers his lies to become a reality in your life.

Hence, the reason you must: *"Clothe yourself with the whole panoply* [the loinbelt, breastplate, shoes and greaves, shield, helmet, sword and lance] *that comes from God, for the sole purpose that you may have explosive and dynamic power to stand proud and upright, face to face and eyeball to eyeball against the roads that the slanderer would try to pave into your mind"* (Ephesians 6:11, REV).

Chapter Four
Wrestling With Principalities And Powers

A S PAUL CONTINUES in the sixth chapter of Ephesians, he reveals who our battle is against. He says, "For we wrestle not against flesh and blood, but against principalities, against powers, against the rulers of the darkness of this world, against spiritual wickedness in high places" (Ephesians 6:12).

Especially notice how Paul begins this verse. He says, "For we *wrestle. . . .*" From the very outset of this verse, Paul makes a very strong, pointed and dramatic statement!

The word "wrestle" is taken from the old word *pale* (pa-le), and it refers to struggling, wrestling, or hand-to-hand fighting. However, the word *pale* is also the Greek word from which the Greek derived their name for the *Palastra* (pa-la-stra), a house of combat sports.

The Palastra was a huge building that outwardly looked like a palace; it was a palace of combat sports, dedicated to the cultivation of athletic skills. Every morning, afternoon and night you could find the most committed, determined and daring athletes of the day working out and training in this fabulous building.

Primarily three kinds of athletes worked out at the Palastra: *boxers, wrestlers and pankratists.* These were exceedingly dangerous and barbaric sports. *Why?* To quote from my book, LIVING IN THE COMBAT ZONE (pages 159-162):

"First, their boxers were not like ours today. Theirs were *extremely violent* — so violent that they were not permitted to box without wearing helmets. Without the protection of helmets, their heads would have been crushed.

"Few boxers in the ancient world ever lived to retire from their profession. Most of them died in the ring. Of all the sports, the ancients viewed boxing as *the most* hazardous and deadly.

"In fact, these boxers were so brutal and barbaric, they wore gloves that were *ribbed with steel and spiked with nails!* At times the steel wrapped around their gloves was *serrated*, like a hunting knife, in order to make deep gashes in the skin of an opponent.

"In addition to this, boxers began using gloves that were heavier and much more damaging. It is quite usual, when viewing the artwork from the time of the early Greeks, to see boxers whose faces, ears, and noses were totally deformed because of these dangerous gloves.

"In studying the art of the Greeks, it is quite usual to see paintings of boxers with blood pouring from their noses and with deep lacerations on their faces as a result of the serrated metal and spiked nails on the gloves. And it was not unusual for a boxer to hit the face so hard, with his thumb extended toward the eyes, that it knocked an eye right out of its socket.

"Believe it or not, even though this sport was so combative and violent, there were *no rules* — except you could not clench your opponent's fist. That was the only rule to the game! There were no "rounds" like there are in boxing today. The fight just went on and on and on until one of the two *surrendered* or *died* in the ring.

"An inscription from that first century said of boxing: 'A boxer's victory is obtained through blood.' This was a thoroughly violent sport!

"Wrestlers, too, often wrestled to the death. In fact, a favorite tactic in those days was to grab hold of an opponent around the waist from behind, throw him up in the air, and quickly break his backbone in half from behind. In order to make an opponent surrender, it was quite normal to strangle him into submission. Choking was another acceptable practice. So wrestling was another extremely violent sport.

"They were tolerant of every imaginable tactic: *breaking fingers, breaking ribs by a waistlock, gouging the face, knocking the eyes out, and so forth.* Although less injurious than the other combat sports, wrestling was still a bitter struggle to the end. . . Wrestling was a bloody, bloody sport.

"Then there were *Pankratists*. Pankratists were a combination of all of the above. The word "pankratist" is from two Greek roots, the words *pan* and *kratos*. *Pan* means "all," and *kratos* is a word for "exhibited power." The two words together describe *'someone with massive amounts of power; power over all; more power than anyone else.'*

"This, indeed, was the purpose of *Pankration*. Its competitors were out to prove they could not be beaten and were tougher than anyone else!

"In order to prove this, they were permitted to kick, punch, bite, gouge, strike, break fingers, break legs, and do any other horrible thing you could imagine. . . There was no part of the body that was off-limits. They could do anything to any part of their competitor's body, *for there were basically no rules.*

"An early inscription says this about *Pankration:* 'If you should hear that your son has died, believe it, but if you hear he has been defeated and retired, do not believe it.' Why? Because more died in this sport than surrendered or were defeated. Like the other combat sports, it was *extremely violent.*"

The Survival of the Fittest

Now Paul uses this very illustration to describe our conflict with unseen, demonic powers that have been marshalled against us for our destruction. He says, "For we wrestle not against flesh and blood, but against principalities, against powers, against the rulers of the darkness of this world, against spiritual wickedness in high places."

By using the word "wrestle," which is the old Greek word *pale*, Paul conveys the idea of a *bitter struggle and an intense conflict* — which describes our warfare with demonic forces as a combat sport!

This means when you are fighting demonic foes, *there are no rules! Anything goes!* All methods of attack are legal, and there is no umpire to cry "foul" when the adversary attempts to break you, choke you, or strangle you.

Whoever fights the hardest, the meanest, and lasts the longest is the winner of this confrontation. Therefore, you'd better be equipped, alert, and prepared before the fight begins! This means putting away sin and being in intimate fellowship with the Holy Spirit and the Word.

Notice that Paul goes on to say, "For our wrestle is *not against flesh and blood. . . .*" At first, this statement from Paul seems to be in conflict with what I have written previously in this book. In this book, I have stated that the majority of spiritual warfare is with the mind and the flesh.

Is there a conflict between me and Paul? *Absolutely not!* Indeed, our real adversary is an unseen host of wicked spirits that are working behind the scenes. These are the foul forces of darkness that work covertly behind every damnable disaster and moral failure. *However, they can't do anything unless your flesh cooperates with them!* Therefore, they come to tempt, seduce, deceive and assault the flesh and the mind.

However, the majority of demonic attacks against us will never produce anything of any serious consequence if we are living a crucified life, and if we are reckoning ourselves to be "dead to sin" (Romans 6:6,7,11).

Thus, the reason that we must deal with the flesh before we attempt to deal with the devil! By living a crucified, sanctified life on a continual basis, we are able to neutralize any attack which the enemy would try to wage against the flesh. Why is this so? *Because dead men and women do not have the capacity to respond!* You can kick dead people, spit at dead people, curse at dead people, try to tempt, deceive and seduce dead people, but they do not respond!

Principalities and Powers

Who are these evil forces that are constantly working behind the scenes to seduce, deceive, control and manipulate the flesh and the mind?

Paul continues, "For we wrestle not against flesh and blood, *but against principalities, against powers, against the rulers of the darkness of this world, against spiritual wickedness in high places.*"

Paul tells us there are four classifications of demon spirits. He says there are (1) *"principalities,"* (2) *"powers,"* (3) *"rulers of the darkness of this world,"* and (4) *"spiritual wickedness in high places."*

Before we deal with each of these individually, first something else must be noted. Notice that Paul mentions the word "against" in Ephesians 6:12 *four times* in connection with the devil! Why is this important? Because grammatically, he could have used the word "against" once in reference to all four of these things. But rather than do this, he chose to repeat the word "against" again, again, again and again.

When a truth is repeated in scripture like this, it is always for the sake of *emphasis.* For instance, in John, chapters fourteen, fifteen and sixteen, Jesus refers to the Holy Spirit as "the Comforter" four different times. This clearly means that the Lord Jesus Christ was trying to drive a very important truth into our hearts about the Holy Spirit.

Likewise, in those same chapters of John, the Lord Jesus Christ refers to the Holy Spirit as "the Spirit of Truth" three different times. Once again, the Lord was repeating Himself for the sake of *emphasizing a very important truth.*

When God calls notable Biblical characters, He always calls them by name not once, but two or three times. For instance, when God called Moses, He said, "*Moses, Moses. . .*" (Exodus 3:4). When God called Saul of Tarsus, He said, "*Saul, Saul. . .*" (Acts 9:4). And Samuel was so important to the plan of God, that when God called Samuel, He called Samuel by name not once, not twice, but three times. God called, "*Samuel. . . Samuel. . . Samuel. . .*" (First Samuel 3:4-8).

So when God is dealing with truth that is of paramount importance, or when God calls an extremely important Biblical character, He always repeats Himself. This, of course, leads us back to Ephesians 6:12, where the Holy Spirit repeats the word "against" *four times* within the context of *one verse!* This means the Holy Spirit is telling us something *very, very, very important.*

The word "against" used all four times in this verse, is taken from the word *pros*. The word *pros* always depicts a "forward position" or a "face-to-face encounter." In fact, this very word is used in John 1:1 to describe the preincarnation relationship between the Father and Jesus. It says, "In the beginning was the Word, and the Word was *with* God. . . ."

The word "with" is taken from the word *pros*. A more accurate rendering of John 1:1 would be, "*In the beginning was the Word [Jesus], and the Word [Jesus] was face to face with God. . . .*"

This is the picture of the Father and Jesus so *intimate* that they can nearly feel their breath breathing upon each other's face. This clearly reveals the *intimacy* and *close relationship* that exists between the members of the Godhead.

Now this same word of intimacy, this word that is used to denote a "face-to-face" relationship between the Father and the Son, is now used to denote a "face-to-face" encounter with unseen, demonic spirits that have come to assault us.

This means at some point in our Christian experience, we will come into *direct contact* with evil forces. The word *pros* in Ephesians 6:12 could be translated, ". . .*face to face with principalities, eyeball to eyeball with powers, head-on with rulers of the darkness of this world, and shoulder to shoulder with spiritual wickedness in high places."*

The Rank and File of the Devil

All serious scholars agree that the language of Ephesians 6:12 is military language. It seems evident that Paul had received a revelation of how Satan's kingdom has been aligned militarily.

At the very top of Satan's dark domain, there is a group of demon spirits whom Paul calls *"principalities."* The word "principality" is taken from the word *archas* (arch-as), an old word that is used symbolically to denote "ancient, ancient times." Furthermore, it is also used to depict individuals who "hold the highest and loftiest position of rank and authority."

By using the word *archas* ("principalities"), Paul emphatically tells us that at the very top of Satan's domain is a group of demon spirits who have held their lofty positions of power and authority since ancient times — probably ever since the fall of Lucifer.

Then Paul continues to mention *"powers"* as those evil forces that are second in command in Satan's dark dominion. The word "powers" is taken from the word *exousia* (ex-ou-sia), and it denotes "delegated authority."

This tells us that there is a lower-ranking group of demon spirits who have received "delegated authority" from Satan to do whatever they want to do, wherever they desire to do it. This second group of demon spirits have "delegated authority" to carry out all manner of evil and wickedness.

Next, Paul mentions *"the rulers of the darkness of this world."* What an amazing word this is! It is taken from the word *kosmokrateros* (kos-mo-kra-te-ros), and is a compound of the words *kosmos* and *kratos*. The word *kosmos* denotes "order" or "arrangement," while the word *kratos* has to do with "raw power."

When these two words are compounded together into the word *kosmokrateros,* they depict "raw power that has been harnessed and put into some kind of order." This word was technically used by the Greek to describe certain aspects of the military.

Why did the ancient Greeks use the word *kosmokrateros* to depict certain aspects of the military? Because the military was filled with young men who had a lot of natural ability — *raw power,* if you will. In order for that raw power to be effective, it had to be harnessed and organized *(kosmos).*

Thus, young soldiers with abounding energy were taught to be submitted, disciplined, ordered and perfectly arranged. *This is the picture of rank and file.* In the end, all of those men, with all of that raw ability, were turned into a massive force.

Now Paul uses this same idea! By using the phrase "rulers of the darkness of this world," he tells us that the devil deals with his dark legions of demon spirits like they are troops! He puts them in rank and file, gives them orders and assignments, and then sends them out like troops who are committed to kill.

It is a fact that we have more authority than the devil. We have more power than the devil. And we have the Greater One living within us. In light of this, one day I asked the Lord, "If we have more authority, and if we have more power, and if we have the Greater One living inside us, then why does it seem that the Church is full of so much defeat?"

I will never forget what the Holy Spirit whispered to my heart. He said, *"The reason the Church is experiencing so much defeat is because the devil has something that the Church does not have!"* I quickly asked, "Lord, what is that?" It was then that the Lord quickened Ephesians 6:12 to my understanding.

The word *kosmokrateros* came alive in my heart, and then I understood!

The word *kosmokrateros* ("rulers of the darkness of this world") is a military term that has to do with *discipline, organization and commitment!*

The devil is so serious about doing damage to humanity, that he deals with demon spirits as though they are *troops!* They are put in rank and file, and are organized to the hilt — *while the average Spirit-filled believer doesn't stay in one church for over one year at a time!*

Yes, we do have more authority than the devil has, and we do have more power than the devil has, and we do have the Greater One living in us. The Church of Jesus Christ is loaded with heaps and heaps of raw power — *but at this particular time, that power is disconnected and disjointed by a body that lacks discipline, organization and commitment!*

The Church of Jesus Christ has no power shortage, nor is the Church short of God-given authority. We simply have a great lack of discipline, organization and commitment. In order to change this, we must buckle down in the local church and begin to view ourselves as the troops of the Lord! *If we will match the discipline, organization and commitment that the enemy has in his camp, then we will begin to move into the awesome demonstration of God's power!*

Finally, Paul mentions *"spiritual wickedness in high places."* The word "wickedness" is taken from the word *poneros* (po-ne-ros), and it is used to depict something that is "bad," "vile," malevolent," "vicious," "impious" or "malignant."

It is important that Paul would save this word until the end of this verse. By saving this phrase until the last, he is telling us the ultimate aim of Satan's dark domain: these spirits are sent forth from the spirit realm to afflict humanity in a "bad, vile, malevolent, vicious, impious and malignant" way.

Chapter Five
Who is the Devil?

A LL SCHOLARS OF THE CHURCH, in the past ages and the present, agree that we have an adversary who hates the gospel, detests the presence of the Church, and is working around the clock to discredit the message of Jesus Christ. Rather than hide from this foe, we must turn our eyes to the Scripture, to see what the Bible has to say about him.

His entrance into the life of a believer is given primarily by way of negligence, as he slips through an uncommitted, unrenewed area of the mind — *a loophole* — and then he begins to wage warfare against the mind and flesh of the saints.

There are many names, symbols and types for the devil throughout the Old and New Testaments. Each of these names, symbols and types reveals a different facet of the devil's twisted, perverted nature, and his mode of operation.

He is known as:

Abaddon (Revelation 9:11)

Accuser (Revelation 12:10)

Adversary (First Peter 5:8)

Angel of Light (Second Corinthians 11:14)

Apollyon (Revelation 9:11)

Beelzebub (Matthew 10:25; 12:24)

Belial (Second Corinthians 6:15)

Devil (Ephesians 6:11; First Peter 5:8; Revelation 12:9)

Dragon (Revelation 12:9)

Evil one (Matthew 6:13)

Murderer (John 8:44)

Prince of this world (John 12:31)

Prince of demons (Matthew 9:34, RSV)

Prince of the power of the air (Ephesians 2:2)

Roaring lion (First Peter 5:8)

Satan (Luke 10:18)

Serpent (Revelation 12:9)

These names, symbols and types of Satan can be divided into four categories: (1) *Satan's Destructive Bent*, (2) *Satan's Perverted Nature*, (3) *Satan's Desire To Control*, and (4) *Satan, the Mind Manipulator*.

Satan's Destructive Bent

Of the seventeen names, symbols and types given above, two are devoted to Satan's insatiable desire to destroy.

The names *Abaddon* and *Apollyon* are found in Revelation 9:11 to describe the devil. The name *Abaddon* is the Hebrew equivalent of the Greek name *Apollyon*. Both of these names mean *"Destroyer."*

In reference to Satan, Revelation 9:11 says, "And they had a king over them, which is the angel of the bottomless pit, whose name in the Hebrew tongue is *Abaddon*, but in the Greek tongue hath his name *Apollyon*."

Possessing his nature and operating on instructions given them by Satan, you can be certain that demon spirits (whom Satan rules over as a king, according to Revelation 9:11), are sent forth with their master's same destructive nature; they are sent forth to "destroy."

Satan's Perverted Nature

Of the titles given in the list above, five of them have to do with the devil's twisted, perverted nature. Those five are found in the following names, symbols and types: *Beelzebub, Belial, Dragon, Evil One,* and *Murderer.*

Beelzebub

The name *Beelzebub* was initially used by the Philistines of the Old Testament to describe the god of Ekron. It literally meant, "lord of the flies" (Second Kings 1:2-6). Originally, it was spelled *Baalzebub.* As time progressed, the Jews altered *Baalzebub* to *Beelzebub,* which added an even dimmer idea to this particular name of the devil. This new name *(Beelzebub)* now meant, "lord of the dunghill," or "lord of the manure."

Two powerful and important images of Satan are presented in these two names. First of all, he is presented as *Baalzebub,* the "lord of the flies." This is clearly the picture of Satan masquerading himself as the lord of demon spirits. Obviously, the Philistines looked upon demon spirits in the same way one would look upon nasty, dirty "flies."

Secondly, he is presented as *Beelzebub,* the "lord of the dunghill." By adding this twist to this name of Satan, the Jews told us something very important about the devil. Both he and his evil spirits, like nasty, dirty flies, are attracted to "dunghills" or environments where rotting, stinking, carnality pervades. This is the environment where Satan thrives best.

Belial

The name *Belial,* which is of Greek origination, means "worthless." This name is always used in connection with filthiness and wickedness. Whenever it is used, either in the Old Testament or the New Testament, it is used to depict extremely evil men. For instance, First Samuel 2:12 tells us that Eli's sons were "sons of *Belial.*"

What an example Eli's sons were of this word *Belial*. They were fornicators, thieves, and were full of idolatry and rebellion. These terrible traits were ingrained into their character to such an extent, that God's judgment came upon them and they were removed from the scene in one day's time. According to First Samuel 2:12, they were "sons of *Belial.*" They obtained this horrid behavior from Satan, who is himself the origination of the word *Belial*.

Dragon

The word *dragon* is also used in Revelation 12:9 to depict the devil. It says, "And the great *dragon* was cast out, that old *serpent*, called the Devil, and Satan, which deceiveth the whole world: he was cast out into the earth, and his angels were cast out with him."

It is clear from this verse that the terms *dragon* and *serpent* are used interchangeably in reference to Satan's twisted, demented and perverted nature. By employing both of these pictures, he is presented as a deadly, poisonous, ready-to-strike-and-kill creature.

Evil One

The next Biblical example of the devil can be found in what is traditionally called "The Lord's Prayer." In Matthew 6:13, the Lord Jesus prayed, "And lead us not into temptation, but deliver us from evil." The Greek language more accurately reads, "but deliver us from the *Evil One.*"

From this usage, we know that Jesus looked upon the devil as the *"Evil One."* No one was more familiar with Satan than Jesus; hence, it is important that Jesus, knowing him so well, would label him thus.

Murderer

It was also the Lord Jesus who told us Satan was a *murderer*. In John 8:44, Jesus told the scribes and Pharisees, "Ye are of your father the devil, and the lusts of your fathers ye will do. He was a *murderer* from the beginning, and abode not in truth. . . ."

This murderous nature of Satan was first manifest in Genesis 4:8, when he inspired Cain to slay his brother, Abel. It was this murderous nature of Satan that inspired Herod to kill all the babies in Bethlehem-Ephrata. We can see his murderous nature in the death of millions of early Christian martyrs, and still today where injustice prevails across the earth. *Murder is a part of his demented nature.*

Satan's Desire To Control

Satan's strong desire to *control* the spirit realm, the world, and every human government and human institution of the world is evidenced by the fact that the Bible calls him *"the prince of this world," "the prince of demons,"* and *"the prince of the power of the air."*

The Prince of this World

By calling him *"the prince of this world,"* even Jesus recognized Satan's temporal control over certain things in this earthly sphere.

You must remember that Satan himself personally offered Jesus the "kingdoms of this world" during Jesus' forty days and nights of testing in the wilderness. Jesus was confronted by this "prince of the world" during those forty days, and resisted the devil's power until he fled. Jesus spoke from personal experience when he referred to this temporal claim of Satan.

The Prince of Demons

In Matthew 9:34, Satan is also called *"the prince of demons."* The word "prince" is taken from the Greek word *archontas* (ar-chon-tas), and refers to "one who holds the first place" or "one who holds the highest seat of power."

The title "prince of demons" most assuredly reveals that Satan holds the highest-ranking seat among many diabolical spirits. The word "prince" denotes that there is some kind of rank and file and organization to Satan's system of things. We have already seen this in Ephesians 6:12.

Prince of the Power of the Air

The apostle Paul called Satan *"the prince of the power of the air"* (Ephesians 2:2). Again, the word "prince" is taken from the Greek word *archontas,* meaning "one who holds the highest seat of power."

This is in complete agreement with Ephesians 6:12, which states that under Satan's control there are varying degrees of spiritually wicked power. From the context of this verse in the sixth chapter of Ephesians, we know that under Satan's command there are principalities, powers, rulers of the darkness of this world, and spiritual wickedness in high places.

Satan, the Mind Manipulator

Finally, we come to the last and largest category of the names, symbols and types of Satan in the Bible. In this last category, we discover that Satan truly is *the master of mind games.*

There are six names, symbols and types of Satan that specifically have to do with his ability to twist, deceive and lie to the mind. He is called the *Adversary, Accuser, Angel of Light, Devil, Roaring Lion,* and *Satan.*

Adversary

The name *Adversary* is extremely important when attempting to understand the devil's mode of operation. It is taken from the Greek word *antidikos* (an-ti-di-kos), which is a compound of the Greek words *anti* (an-ti) and *dikos* (di-kos).

The word *anti* simply means "against." However, in older and more classical Greek, it was used to denote the mental condition of a man or woman who was "on the edge of insanity." This, in fact, was a terribly dangerous person who would do someone great harm if he or she was not restrained. Therefore, the word *anti* is quite a nasty word.

The second part of the word *Adversary* is taken from the Greek word *dikos. Dikos* is the root for the word "righteousness." It refers to "justice, rightness, fairness, and righteousness."

When the two words are compounded together, they portray "one who is adamantly opposed to righteousness." Because the word *anti* carries the idea of hostility, this means the devil is one who is "hostile toward righteousness" or "he is one who desires to destroy righteousness and obliterate it."

This means the devil is not just passively opposed to the presence of righteousness or righteous people; *he is actively pursuing them and doing all within his power to wipe them out!* He *hates* righteousness!

In one way or another, he mentally tries to devour them with temptation of the present, or with memories of the past. All of this is done by him in order to assault our sense of righteousness, in the hopes that we will be left high and dry with no confidence before God, devil or man.

This is precisely why Peter said, "Be sober, be vigilant; because your *adversary* the devil, as a roaring lion, walketh about, seeking whom he may devour" (First Peter 5:8).

A Roaring Lion

And this leads us to the next title of Satan. Peter says he is like unto *"a roaring lion."* What awesome command the roar of a lion draws from the heart of frail man!

In this case, the roar is more fearsome than his bite. Colossians 2:15 victoriously declares, "And having spoiled principalities and powers, he made a shew of them openly, triumphing over them in it."

By means of the cross and the resurrection, Jesus Christ stripped these demonic powers bare of the authority they once possessed, and His victory over them was so thorough that he even "made a shew of them openly," bringing them down in complete humiliation and total defeat.

However, this has not stopped the devil from trying to sound dreadful. It is his continuous hassling of our thoughts, his insinuations about failure, his concoction of unrealistic fears in our souls, and his constant onslaught against our minds that beats believers down into defeat. This constant "roaring" in the soul is another attempt of the adversary to wear us out, wear us down, and then swallow us up in self-pity.

Notice that the object of the adversary is to *"seek those whom he may devour."* The word "seek" implies that not everyone will fall prey to these tactics.

He is not seeking *anyone* whom he may devour; he is seeking *those* whom he may devour — *he is looking for those who are weak in faith, ignorant of the Word of God, who are isolated to themselves, and are not mature enough to stand in the face of his constant, hassling allegations.*

These are the ones that this "roaring lion" is seeking after, and his object is to *"devour them."* The word "devour" comes from the Greek word *katapino* (ka-ta-pi-no), and literally means "to swallow up completely."

Angel of Light

And, of course, Satan is called an *"angel of light."* In Second Corinthians, Paul, dealing with the problem of false prophets, false teachers, false apostles and deceivers who were trying to worm their way into the Corinthian Church, says, "And no marvel; for Satan himself is transformed into an angel of light" (Second Corinthians 11:14).

This is another picture of this master mind-manipulator; Satan disguises himself to be something that he really is not! Again, this kind of attack normally comes against the mind. This is a vivid portrayal of Satan's deceptive power to twist one's thinking.

The Devil

And, of course, Satan is also called *"the devil."* As a matter of fact, the New Testament refers to him as such over forty times!

As we saw earlier in Chapter Three, the name *"devil"* is taken from the Greek word *diabolos* (di-a-bo-los). It is a

compound of the words *dia* and *balos*. *Dia* means "through" and carries with it the idea of "penetration." The word *balos* is taken from the word *ballo*, which means "I throw," as in throwing a ball or a rock.

When the two words are compounded, they depict the act of repeatedly throwing a ball or rock against something until it penetrates that barrier, and breaks through to the other side.

Therefore, in the name "*devil*," you do not only have the proper name of this archenemy, but also his mode of operation. His name means that he is "one who continually strikes, strikes and strikes again — beating against the walls of our minds over and over, and over and over again — until finally, he breaks through and penetrates" the mind.

Satan

And last, this enemy of both God and man is called *Satan*, which is taken from the Hebrew word *shatana*, and means "to hate and to accuse." It is used more than fifty times in the Old and New Testament, and often it also carries with it the ideas of "slander and false accusation."

A Prerequisite to Spiritual Warfare

It was because of this archenemy that Paul wrote to the Ephesian Church and urged them to "put on the whole armor of God" (Ephesians 6:11).

However, before he told them to "put on the whole armor of God," he urged them "to put away lying" (4:25); "to speak truth with our neighbor" (4:25); he commanded them, "be ye angry, and sin not: let not the sun go down upon your wrath" (4:26); "neither give place to the devil" (4:27); "let him that stole steal no more" (4:28); "let no corrupt communication proceed out of your mouth" (4:29); "grieve not the Holy Spirit" (4:30); "let all bitterness, and wrath, and anger, and clamour, and evil speaking, be put away from you, with all malice" (4:31).

We must not forget that a consecrated life is a prerequisite to real spiritual warfare. If these areas of our lives are left unattended, uncommitted and unsurrendered, then we have left gaping loopholes through which Satan may continue to exert his hellish schemes in our lives.

Screaming, yelling, screeching, stomping, shouting, and dancing will not accomplish one single thing if we have (deliberately, or simply by negligence) allowed "the loins of our minds" to go unchecked and ungirded. Our lack of commitment to God's Word and the secret places of our lives that have never been fully surrendered to Jesus Christ will stop us dead in our tracks when it comes to dealing with the devil's attacks.

On the other hand, a holy and surrendered man, who has carefully guarded his mind and has equipped himself with the *whole armor of God, is an awesome weapon in the hands of an Almighty God!*